Deep in the Sea

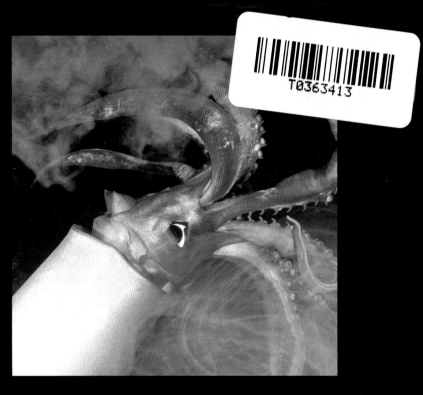

Written by Patrick Lay

Contents

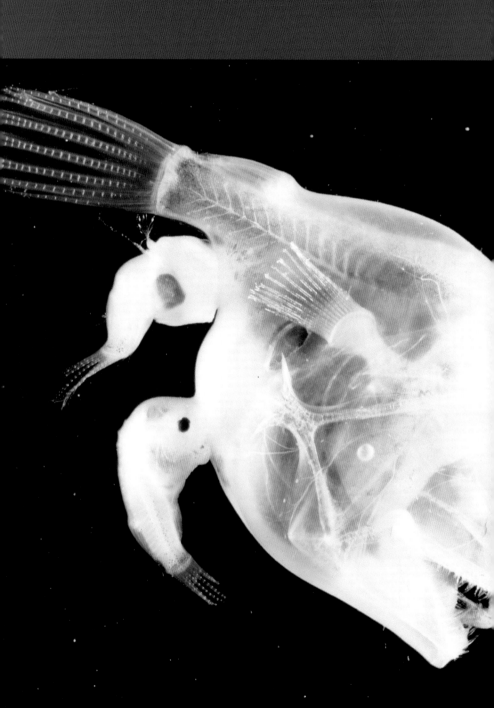

Introduction

Deep in the sea, it is very dark and the water is freezing cold.

Animals that live deep in the sea have clever ways of getting food and staying safe. They use their big eyes, huge mouths, lights and colour to help them do these things.

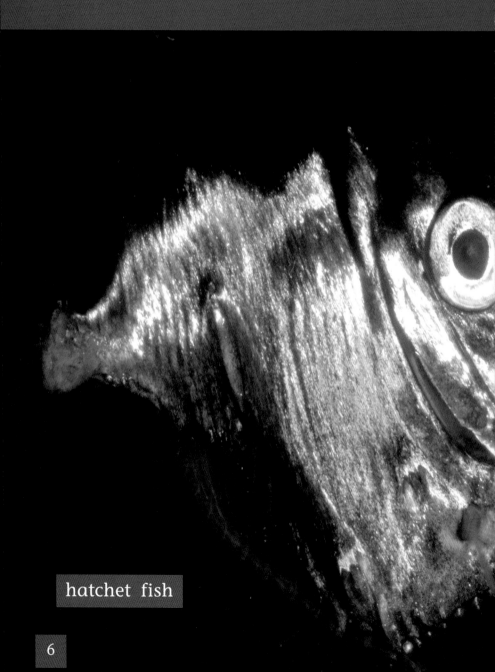

hatchet fish

Chapter 1 Big eyes

Some animals that live deep in the sea have big eyes. This helps them to see in the dark water.

This fish has very big eyes. It also has lights on its tail and on its underside. Its big eyes and these lights help the fish to see in the dark.

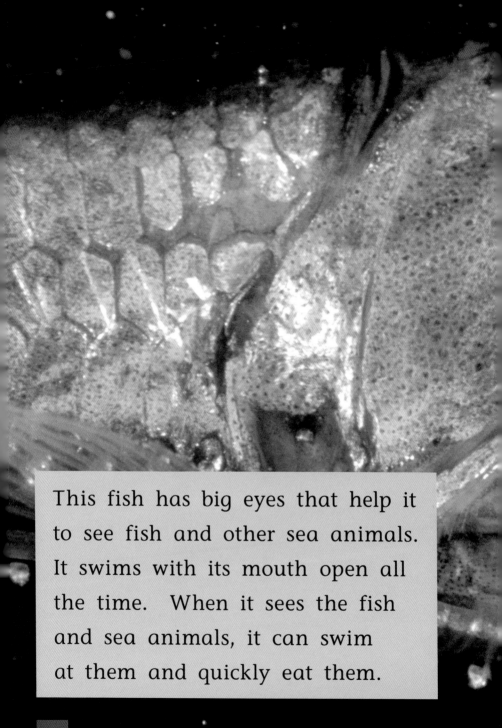

This fish has big eyes that help it to see fish and other sea animals. It swims with its mouth open all the time. When it sees the fish and sea animals, it can swim at them and quickly eat them.

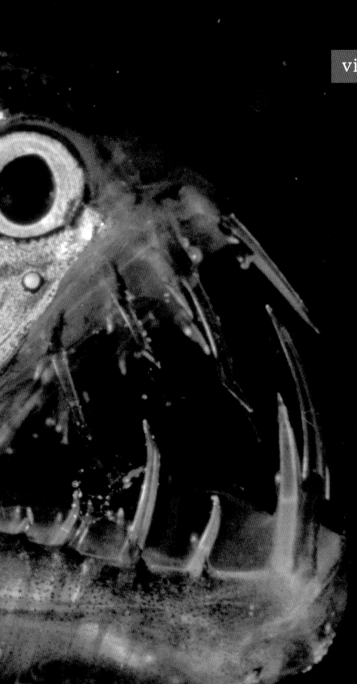

This is a giant squid. It can grow to almost 18 metres long. It has enormous eyes about the size of a person's head.

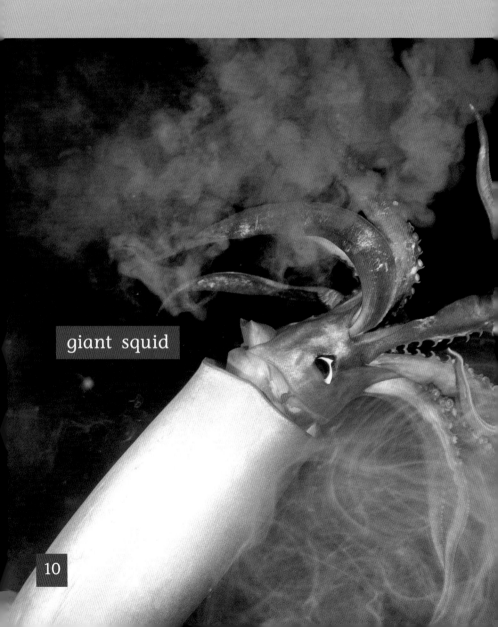

giant squid

fangtooth fish

Chapter 2

Huge mouth

Some animals in the deep sea have huge mouths. This helps them to trap other animals to eat.

This fish has huge jaws with sharp, pointy teeth like fangs. When other animals come close, the fish opens its mouth wide and snaps its jaws shut to trap them.

gulper eel

This fish can open its jaws wide to catch animals to eat. Its insides are so stretchy that it can eat animals that are as big as itself.

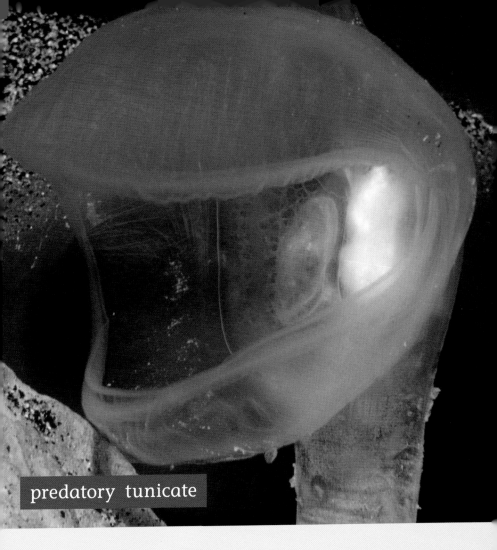

predatory tunicate

This animal is attached to the bottom of the sea floor. It cannot swim away to catch food. It traps sea animals in its huge mouth as they swim past.

deep sea dragonfish

Chapter 3 Lights on

Some animals that live in the deep sea are able to make their own light. This light helps the animals to see in the dark. The light also attracts other small sea animals for them to eat.

This fish has a long barb. The barb has a light on the end of it. The light attracts other fish that can then be eaten.

lantern fish

This fish has lots of lights on its head, tail and underside. These lights attract other small fish for it to eat.

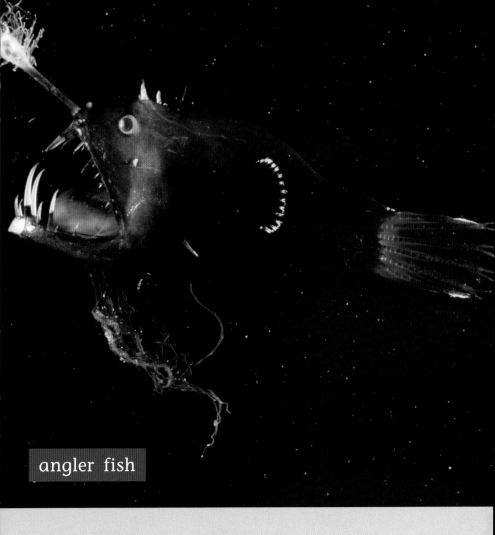

angler fish

This fish has a spine that hangs down over its mouth. A light on the end of this spine attracts other fish. Then the fish eats them.

big, red jellyfish

Chapter 4 Colour

Deep in the sea, it is hard to see the colour red. Animals that are red look black and other animals cannot see them.

This big, red jellyfish looks black to other animals. It drifts along without being seen and eats tiny sea animals.

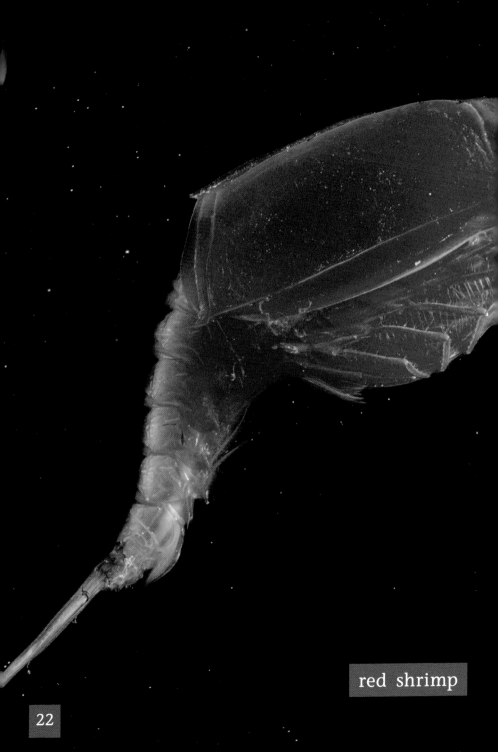

red shrimp

This red shrimp can squirt out a glowing liquid if a fish comes near it. This confuses the fish and gives the shrimp a chance to get away.

Index